How

WINDSURF

a step·by·step guide

Author:
Liz French

Technical consultant:
Mike Nutt
RYA qualified instructor,
British team member,
Windsurfer Class
European
Championships
1982-87

JARROLD

Other titles in this series are:

TENNIS   **SWIMMING**
SQUASH   **GOLF**
BADMINTON   **SNOOKER**
CROQUET   **DINGHY SAILING**
BOWLS   **GET FIT FOR SPORT**
TABLE TENNIS

How to WINDSURF
ISBN 0-7117-0503-8
First published in Great Britain, 1990
Text copyright © Liz French, 1990
This edition copyright © 1990 Jarrold Publishing
Illustrations by Malcolm Ryan

Designed and produced by
Parke Sutton Limited, Norwich
for Jarrold Publishing, Norwich

Contents

Introduction

Windsurfing is the UK's fastest-growing sport. Here is sailing at its most elementary – and, perhaps, its most exhilarating. Certainly, no other sport brings you into closer contact with the powers of wind and water.

The best way to begin is to take an introductory course at any one of the many windsurfing centres around the country, both on inland waters and on the coast. Here you will receive expert tuition and within a few hours experience the thrill of gliding through the water for the first time. Contact the Royal Yachting Association for details at RYA House, Romsey Road, Eastleigh, Hants SO5 4YA.

You will need to understand the basics of technique before you can progress very far with windsurfing. This book explains all the essential points, including safety procedures, developing sailing techniques, recognising wind conditions and sailing in stronger winds. The terminology of sailing can be confusing to beginners. In the pages that follow you will find equipment fully explained and any other new terms will be in *italics* when they are mentioned for the first time. Usually an explanation is given at that point in the text, but turn to the glossary at the back for a fuller description if you are not sure of any term.

Once you have mastered the basic skills you may wish to pursue one of the windsurfing specialities — racing, freestyle and wave riding or jumping — which are touched on only very briefly in this book. Advanced courses are offered at many centres, and for the adventurous the potential is almost unlimited.

As a newcomer to windsurfing, you will be joining an ever-growing band of fellow enthusiasts of all ages captivated by this uniquely challenging sport. Happy sailing!

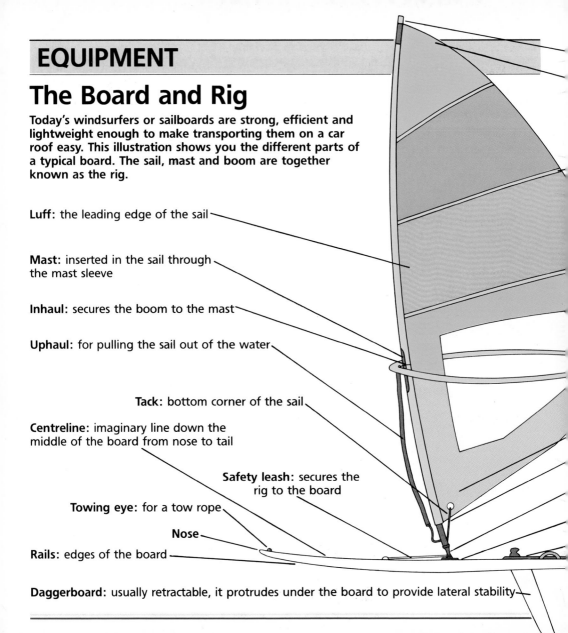

The Board and Rig

Today's windsurfers or sailboards are strong, efficient and lightweight enough to make transporting them on a car roof easy. This illustration shows you the different parts of a typical board. The sail, mast and boom are together known as the rig.

Luff: the leading edge of the sail

Mast: inserted in the sail through the mast sleeve

Inhaul: secures the boom to the mast

Uphaul: for pulling the sail out of the water

Tack: bottom corner of the sail

Centreline: imaginary line down the middle of the board from nose to tail

Safety leash: secures the rig to the board

Towing eye: for a tow rope

Nose

Rails: edges of the board

Daggerboard: usually retractable, it protrudes under the board to provide lateral stability

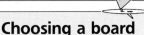

Mast tip

Head: top of the sail

Battens: to keep the sail's shape

Leech: trailing edge of the sail

Clew: back corner of the sail

Outhaul: for pulling the sail taut horizontally

Boom: for holding the rig and altering its position for steering; attached to the mast and the clew

Foot: the bottom edge of the sail

Downhaul: for pulling the sail taut vertically

Mast foot: joins the mast to the track; it has a flexible universal joint (UJ) so that the mast can tilt at any angle

Mast track: allows the mast position to be adjusted (some boards have a fixed socket)

Daggerboard casing

Footstraps: for use in stronger winds (not all boards have them)

Tail

Skeg: smaller fin for directional stability

Choosing a board

Most beginners learn on hired equipment, so this book does not attempt to tell you all about the different types of board available. There are three main kinds of board — long, medium and short. Long boards include types for beginners, general recreation or course racing. In the medium-length category are the slalom boards, while short boards are for wave and speed sailing in high wind conditions. A long funboard is probably the most suitable for learning and is flexible enough to develop freestyle skills.

When you want to buy your own board, ask advice from a qualified tutor or specialist shop. They will also give advice on transporting and caring for your equipment. Basic rigging instruction is given on pages 14-15. The RYA offers a helpful leaflet on choosing a board.

Clothing

In all but the warmest conditions, a well-fitting wetsuit or drysuit is vital to protect yourself from serious wind-chilling. The variety available can be baffling: read magazine reviews, shop around and ask other users. What you will need depends on when, where and for how long you will be wearing the suit.

Wetsuits

Made of a material called neoprene, these are close-fitting and usually worn over swimwear. A wetsuit works by trapping a layer of water which acts as an insulator next to your skin.

For cold weather a heavyweight wetsuit, or steamer, is best. This keeps out 80% of the water. Note the high collar. For warmer weather a lighter weight steamer will be adequate. Arms and legs are often removable. Another versatile option is a longjohn wetsuit with separate jacket. In really warm conditions a 'shortie' wetsuit or neoprene vest may be enough.

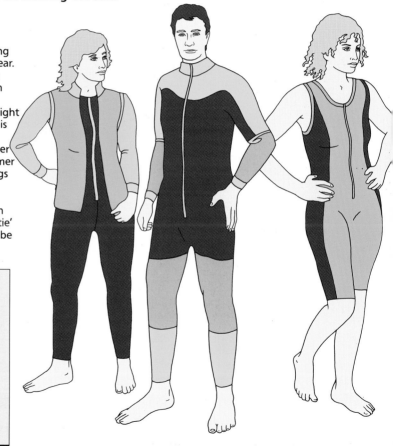

Care of your wetsuit

● Always rinse thoroughly in fresh water after use.
● Dry (away from heat) and store on a hanger.
● Repairs: you can mend small snags yourself with a special kit or simply with rubber adhesive. Larger tears should be repaired by a specialist.

Drysuits

These are the warmest — and most expensive — option. As the name suggests, they are designed to keep you completely dry, with tightly fitting seals at the neck, wrists and ankles (indeed feet are often attached to the leggings). You can wear clothing under a drysuit and the arms and legs are loose to allow freedom of movement.

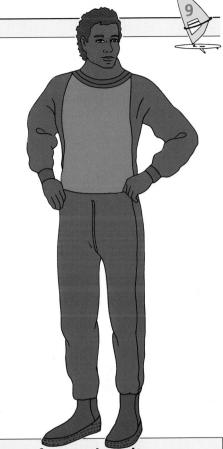

Venting

Make sure you know how to vent your drysuit — that is, to expel excess air — by stretching the neck seal with your fingers and crouching down. This is vital for your safety as trapped air inside the suit makes it hard to get up if you fall in the water.

Care of your drysuit

● Always rinse thoroughly in fresh water after use.
● Dry (away from heat) and store on a hanger.
● Apply talcum powder to the seals to help keep them supple.
● Treat zips with beeswax or candle-wax to keep them running smoothly.

Hats

About a third of body heat loss is from the head and you will feel warmer all over if you wear a hat. Choose a neoprene or other snug-fitting type to wear in cooler conditions.

Gloves

Hands also suffer badly in the cold and it won't help your sailing skills if your hands are too numb to grip! Specialist gloves of neoprene are available but expensive. Ordinary household rubber gloves tucked into the cuffs of your suit are a cheap alternative and reduce windchill — buy a size larger and wear silk motorcyclists' under-gloves inside. If it is blisters you want to avoid, try dinghy sailors' gloves, available from yacht chandlers.

Boots

Some suits have attached boots. Otherwise, a long pair of waterproof boots or soled socks to wear under your suit is advised. When choosing boots, look for durability, good insulation and non-slip soles.

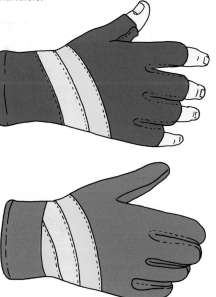

Accessories

A browse round the specialist shop will reveal a wide variety of non-essential accessories from waterproof watches to personal stereos. These are largely a matter of personal choice.

Buoyancy aids

Wearing some kind of buoyancy aid is highly recommended: some centres insist on this. A harness (see page 36) has a degree of buoyancy but is not a life-saving device since it will not support you in a face-up float. Choose from a wide variety of aids: go for one with more buoyancy in front than in the back to allow you to float face-up.

Knapsacks and bumbags

These are available to wear on your back or hips — fill them with the safety items listed on pages 12-13.

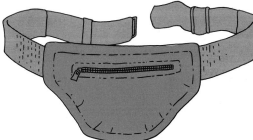

Sunglasses and visors

On bright days you will need to protect your eyes from glare. Ordinary sunglasses will do but make sure they fit securely or tie around your neck. Visors are an alternative option and keep the sun off the top of your face.

Sun tan lotion

Exposed skin can easily get badly burnt because of the glare of the sun off the water. Always use a high-protection, waterproof sun tan lotion.

Safety Sense

Checklist

- How strong is the wind? Beginners should not sail if it is more than Force 3 (see page 45).
- Is the wind blowing away from the shore? Offshore winds are deceptive because the water can look calm. Beginners should NEVER sail in *offshore winds*.
- Is there a strong tide? If you can see water swirling around buoys and posts, there may be dangerous currents. Always heed warning notices. NEVER underestimate the strength of tides (see page 44).
- Have you checked that your equipment is suitable and properly rigged (see checklist opposite)?
- Is your safety pack in your knapsack (see opposite)?
- Have you told someone where you are going and when you will be back? Don't forget to tell them when you return.
- Are you near others? Always sail with a friend or with others nearby — more fun as well as safer.

Self rescue

If your equipment breaks or conditions change, you may be unable to sail back to shore. A standard self-rescue procedure is given here: practise it regularly. As a last resort, use the approved signal for help (see opposite).

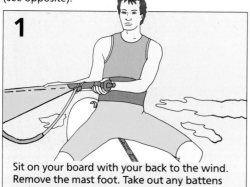

1 Sit on your board with your back to the wind. Remove the mast foot. Take out any battens and put them up the mast sleeve or down your wetsuit.

2 Release the outhaul and push the end of the boom to the top of the mast. The sail can now be tightly rolled towards the mast. Use the uphaul and outhaul to tie the boom and sail to the mast.

3

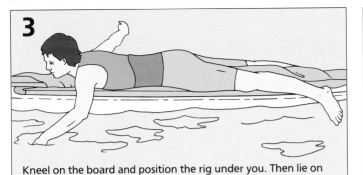

Kneel on the board and position the rig under you. Then lie on top of it and paddle back to shore.

If you have to signal for help:

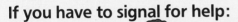

● Slowly raise and lower your arms by your sides. This is the International Distress Signal.

● Stay with your board: it will help keep you afloat and make you easier to spot.

● Use your flares, day-glo flag and whistle if you have them.

● Above all, stay calm.

Equipment checklist

● Make sure your equipment is adequate: in the UK this usually means a wetsuit or drysuit even in summer.

● Check that your gear is in good condition and properly rigged (see pages 14-15).

● If you are hiring equipment, it should be in good order, but do check for and report any signs of damage. Are there signs of wear on the ropes or mast fittings? Is the boom at the right height for you and securely fastened to the sail?

Safety pack

As you become more experienced and are sailing further afield, a knapsack is a sensible addition.

These are sensible items to keep in it:

● two flares: even in bad visibility these will be seen from a long distance

● a whistle: sound travels well over water

● a day-glo flag: waving this back and forth is a recognised distress signal

● rope: for towing or being towed

● a knife

Rigging

You will probably be using ready-rigged hired equipment at first, but it is useful to learn the principles of *rigging*. The detail will vary enormously for different boards, but the basic sequence is usually the same. Ask your instructor or retailer if in doubt.

1

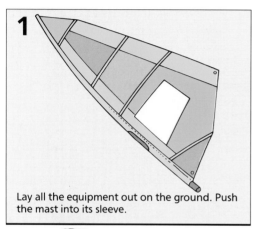

Lay all the equipment out on the ground. Push the mast into its sleeve.

2

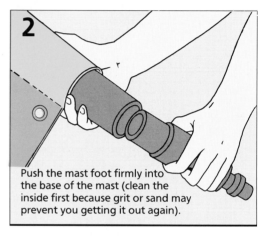

Push the mast foot firmly into the base of the mast (clean the inside first because grit or sand may prevent you getting it out again).

3

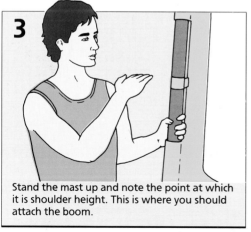

Stand the mast up and note the point at which it is shoulder height. This is where you should attach the boom.

4

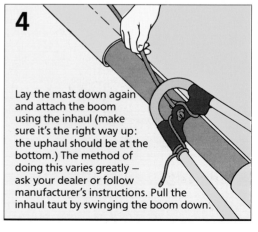

Lay the mast down again and attach the boom using the inhaul (make sure it's the right way up: the uphaul should be at the bottom.) The method of doing this varies greatly — ask your dealer or follow manufacturer's instructions. Pull the inhaul taut by swinging the boom down.

5

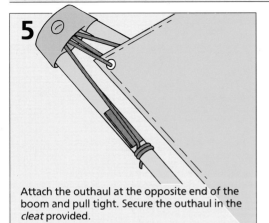

Attach the outhaul at the opposite end of the boom and pull tight. Secure the outhaul in the *cleat* provided.

6

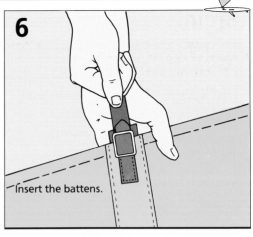

Insert the battens.

7

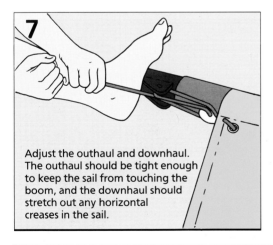

Adjust the outhaul and downhaul. The outhaul should be tight enough to keep the sail from touching the boom, and the downhaul should stretch out any horizontal creases in the sail.

8

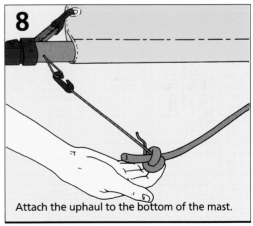

Attach the uphaul to the bottom of the mast.

De-rigging

The order should always be: **BATTENS – DOWNHAUL – OUTHAUL**
You can damage the sail if you try to remove the outhaul first.

Carrying the Board and Rig

It is advisable to carry the board and rig separately. Here are some suggestions for making it easier.

The board

Put the board on its rails with the deck towards you. Stand between the daggerboard slot and mast track. Then lift the board with one hand in the daggerboard slot on the underside of the board, taking most of the weight, and the other in the mast socket to balance.

The rig

You can use the wind to help you carry the rig. Position the rig on the ground at right angles to the wind. Stand behind the mast with your back to the wind. Place one hand on the boom and the other on the mast just above the boom and lift the rig to waist height.
Once you get to the water, it is safer to carry the rig in first as it is less likely to drift away than the board. Then go back for the board.

NOTE: If your board has a retractable daggerboard (see pages 6-7) check that it is in the down position when in the water. It is only retracted for more advanced, stronger wind sailing (see page 30).

Getting the Feel

Everyone falls off at first – don't let this bother you. To improve your balance in the early stages, it is a good idea to leave the rig on the beach for a while and use just the board to get a feel for how it responds to your movements and the water. Make sure the water is calm and there are no strong currents. Remember to keep the daggerboard in the down position.

1 Get on and sit astride the board, tipping it from side to side to see how it responds to your movements.

2 Try walking first to one end and then the other.

3 Turn around a few times in the middle of the board.

4 Try jumping on the board – first on the spot and then with quarter, half and full turns.

What if . . . you can't keep your balance?

Your bodyweight must always be over the centreline. If your feet are over to one side, lean the other way to compensate.

Climbing On

1 As a beginner you will probably be hiring equipment and this will be supplied already rigged (if not, see pages 14-15). Connect the rig to the board by placing the mast foot firmly in its socket or track and attaching the safety leash.

2

Put the board into thigh-deep water at right angles to the wind. The mast should be roughly perpendicular to the board and the daggerboard fully down. Place your hands on either side of the mast socket, on the centreline and about shoulder-width apart.

3

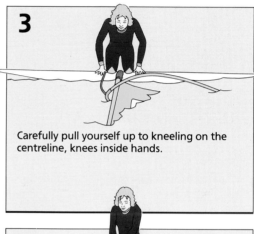

Carefully pull yourself up to kneeling on the centreline, knees inside hands.

4

Clasp the uphaul and move gently into a crouching position with your feet still on the centreline, one each side of the mast foot.

5

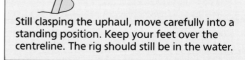

Still clasping the uphaul, move carefully into a standing position. Keep your feet over the centreline. The rig should still be in the water.

Raising the Rig

You will find it helpful to practise on dry land at first.

1

Re-check that the board is at right angles to the wind (start again if it has moved).

2

From the standing position, pull the uphaul taut with both hands. The rig is still in the water.

3

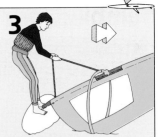

Bend your legs, then straighten them as you pull the sail out of the water, slowly, pausing to let the water drain off. It is important to keep your back straight to avoid strain.

4

Keep pulling the rig up, hand over hand. The board may move as the sail fills with air. Keeping your knees bent will help you balance.

5

With the rig clear of the water, move your hands to the mast and relax, your arms and legs slightly bent. Note the 'V' made by your body and the mast.

6

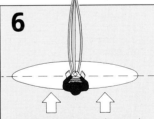

The position you are in now is the most stable position with the board at rest. The wind is behind you and the sail flaps straight ahead. This is known as the *secure position*.

What if . . . you fall off with the rig on the same side as the wind?

The easiest *windward uphauling* method is to pull up the rig slightly so that the clew is still in the water and the board slowly starts to turn. When the sail is on the *leeward* side again, continue from stage 3 above.

Turning Round

The thrill of sailing forward is intoxicating, but before you sail off you need to know how to turn round again. Practise turning the board completely round in both directions. It should be a smooth, relaxed movement. While you are learning the manoeuvre, it is safest to turn in the direction of the wind, otherwise you may find yourself blown *downwind.*

1

Hold the mast in the secure position and tilt it towards the tail of the board. As you tilt the sail, the board turns the other way and into the wind.

2

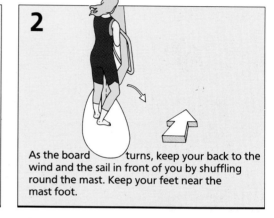

As the board turns, keep your back to the wind and the sail in front of you by shuffling round the mast. Keep your feet near the mast foot.

3

At the end of the turn you should be back in the secure position with your feet equally spaced either side of the mast foot, your back to the wind and facing the opposite direction.

What if . . . you keep falling in?

First, check that you are keeping the movement of the sail smooth and that your body is still making a 'V' with the mast (see page 19). Otherwise, it's likely to be your eyes and/or feet at fault. Eyes: should watch the sail, not your feet. Feet: are your steps too big? You should shuffle gently round the mast. Think of 'scooping' the air with your sail as you turn.

Swinging rig practice

To get a feel for how moving the rig affects the board's movements, practise tilting the rig slowly from the secure position, first into the wind and then back the other way, without completing a full turn.

Sailing Away

Now comes the excitement of moving off. This sequence shows you how to sail straight across the wind on a *beam reach* course. First, from the secure position (see page 19), your back to the wind, choose a spot ahead to aim for. Make sure the sail is at right angles to the board.

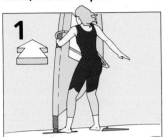

1 Take the *back hand* off the mast. Move your rear foot back over the daggerboard casing, and your *front foot* back behind the mast, pointing towards the nose.

2 Twist your upper body to face your goal, and pull the rig across your body until it feels weightless (the *balance point*).

3 Now put your back hand onto the boom and pull the sail in gently until just full of air — this is known as *sheeting in*.

4 Transfer your other hand to the boom so your hands are shoulder width apart. Lean back with your weight on your back foot to balance the pull of the sail. This is the *sailing position*.

5 To slow down and stop, let go with your back hand and return both hands to the mast in the secure position.

What if . . .
. . .you feel you are about to fall in?

If falling forwards, reduce the sail power by *easing* (or *sheeting*) *out* with your back hand. Or, return to the secure position, putting first your back hand and then the front back on the mast. If falling backwards, pull the sail in with your back hand and quickly bend your knees to bring your weight back over the centreline.

Steering

When you are moving, you steer in the same way as when you practised swinging the rig (see page 19) from the secure position.

Into the wind

From the sailing position (see page 21) identify a spot to aim for *upwind* of the old one. Lean the rig back across your body towards the tail in a smooth movement initiated by extending your back arm. Lean on your back foot. The nose starts to turn into the wind, or to *luff up*.

When the board is facing the new goal, lean the rig forward and regain sailing position. Sheet in slightly with your back hand to keep the sail full. You are now sailing on a *close reach* course.

Away from the wind

Again from the sailing position, pick a spot downwind. Draw the rig forwards across your body by extending your front arm. Lean on your front foot. The nose starts to *bear away* from the wind.

When the board is facing the new goal, return to sailing position. Ease out slightly with your back hand to keep the sail full. You are now sailing on a *broad reach* course.

Check Your Stance

Even in the early stages the way you stand is important — it could be the difference between staying on and falling in. So check that you have it right. This stance is appropriate in light winds: in stronger winds you should keep your weight lower and further back from the board (see page 30).

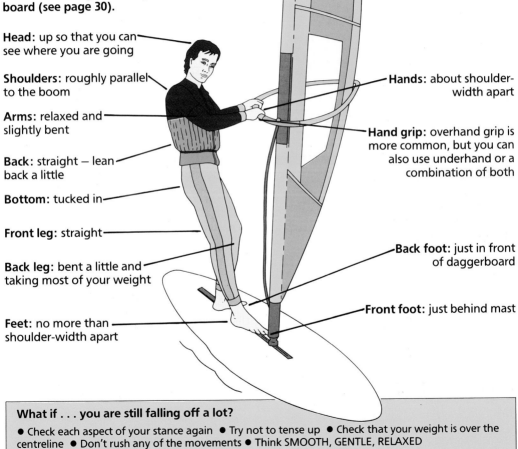

Head: up so that you can see where you are going

Shoulders: roughly parallel to the boom

Arms: relaxed and slightly bent

Back: straight — lean back a little

Bottom: tucked in

Front leg: straight

Back leg: bent a little and taking most of your weight

Feet: no more than shoulder-width apart

Hands: about shoulder-width apart

Hand grip: overhand grip is more common, but you can also use underhand or a combination of both

Back foot: just in front of daggerboard

Front foot: just behind mast

What if . . . you are still falling off a lot?
● Check each aspect of your stance again ● Try not to tense up ● Check that your weight is over the centreline ● Don't rush any of the movements ● Think SMOOTH, GENTLE, RELAXED

Sailing Upwind

Look at this diagram. You have already learned how to sail on a beam reach course and how to steer into a close reach or broad reach (page 22). But what if you want to sail directly into the wind? The answer is, you can't. You will see on the diagram that for about 45° on either side of the wind there is a *No Go Zone.* If you try to sail here, the sail will flap and you will stop or go backwards and probably fall in.

What you can do is sail on a *close-hauled* course — that is, as close to the wind as possible — and *tack* in a zig-zag path towards your upwind goal, passing first through one side of the No Go Zone and then the other. Sailing upwind is also known as *beating.*

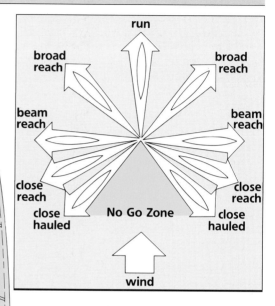

Get on a close-hauled course

To sail a close-hauled course, first follow the sequence for a close reach on page 22 (Into the wind). Then repeat the sequence starting from the close reach position and you will find yourself sailing a close-hauled course on the edge of the No Go Zone.

Tacking

This is by far the quickest and most effective method of sailing upwind. It will take some practice!

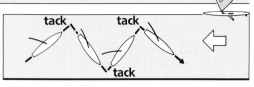

1

Start in the sailing position on a close-hauled course. Move your front hand onto the mast and your front foot just in front of the mast.

2

Lean the rig towards the tail of the board and the board starts to turn. As the nose moves into the wind, move your back hand onto the mast. Quickly and smoothly, step around the mast.

3

When you are standing on the new side of the sail, lean the rig towards the nose until the board is at right angles to the wind, then resume the secure position.

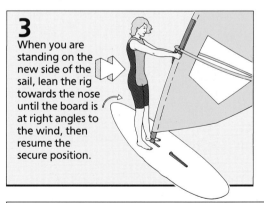

4

Sail off and steer back onto a close-hauled reach. Repeat the sequence to head towards your target.

What if . . . you don't seem to make much progress towards your goal?

You are probably bearing away from the wind too much between tacks. This will make you go faster but you will make less progress upwind. Try to stay on a close-hauled course between tacks.

Sailing Downwind

Now you need to learn to sail with the wind behind you. Sailing with the wind directly behind you is known as *running*. Anything between a run and a beam reach is called a broad reach.

Sail on a run

Steering

1

Starting from a broad reach position (see page 22), tilt the mast forward and sheet out with your back hand.

2

Once the board is on its new course, pull the rig towards you with your front hand.

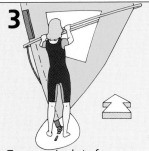

3

Turn your body to face forward, shifting your feet until they're either side of the centreline.

4

When the board is pointing directly downwind, sheet out fully so the sail is at right angles to the board. You are now sailing on a run.

To turn left: either tilt the rig to the right or lean on your right foot – for a quick turn, do both.

To turn right: either tilt the rig to the left or lean on your left foot – again, do both for a quicker response.

Gybing

You already know how to tack, turning the nose of the board into and through the wind. *Gybing* is the opposite kind of turn: here it is the tail which points into and then through the wind. There are many different ways of gybing, all requiring plenty of practice. This sequence shows the easiest and most basic gybe, suitable for light wind. Practise on smooth water. A more advanced gybe is described on pages 34-35.

2

Wind pressure will push the clew of the sail round the nose and make the board start to turn. As it does so, release the boom by taking your front hand off it. To exaggerate the turn, lean the mast away from the direction of the turn.

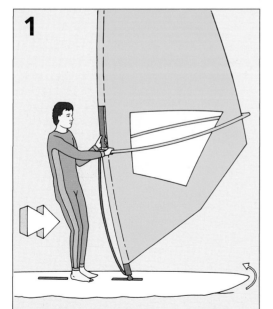

1

Start by sailing on a run. Lean back a little to help your balance. Transfer your back hand from the boom onto the mast.

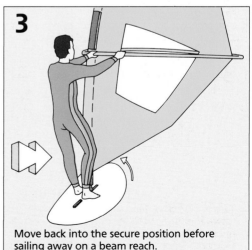

3

Move back into the secure position before sailing away on a beam reach.

Returning to Shore

The obvious rule when coming ashore is to be aware of any swimmers and other beach users: even a slow-moving board can cause injury. A badly controlled return can also damage your board and sail, so do take care.

1

As you approach the shore, but still in knee-deep water, sheet out to slow down and stop in the secure position.

2

Lower the rig onto the water and dismount by stepping off backwards.

3

Separate the rig from the board and carry the board up the beach, returning for the rig.

Board Handling Exercises

Now that you have learned how to sail in any direction in light winds, try these exercises to see how well you have mastered the basic skills.

Rig control

1. Try sailing with your hands as close together as possible – stylish and efficient technique used by top sailors.

2. With your hands together, find the balance point on the boom, then let go with your back hand for a few seconds. Repeat with your front hand.

Feet position

1. Experiment with the position of your feet. Move forward or back to find the optimum sailing speed, and try a narrower stance – less secure but more stylish.

2. As you sail along, lift one foot up and wave it around or trail it in the water. Repeat with the other foot.

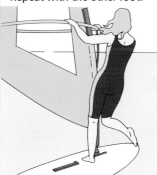

Body position

1. While sailing on a beam reach, crouch down until your arms are fully extended with the boom above your head. Hold the position as long as you can.

2. Sailing on a run, try sitting or kneeling on the board. Try steering in this position.

Mark rounding

Find a buoy and practise rounding it as close as possible. First approach it from upwind and tack around it (diagram A). Then try approaching from downwind and gybing round it (diagram B).

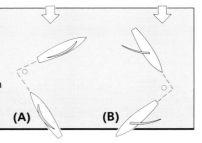

(A)　　　**(B)**

Stopping

Practise stopping quickly by backing the sail: sheet out then push your back hand away from you until the wind fills the back of the sail.

Stronger Wind Techniques

When you can confidently handle the board through all the basic manoeuvres, you will be ready for the challenge of slightly stronger winds. You will find that the board not only travels faster but behaves differently too, so you'll need to adapt your technique. If your board has a retractable daggerboard, it can be partially or even fully retracted now to increase speed on certain courses.

Stance

You'll need to adapt your body position in stronger winds, too. The general rules are:
● bend more at the hips and knees to keep your body weight low   ● lean back with straight arms pulling the mast down over your body   ● position your feet further back and to windward to prevent the board *railing* up.

Starting up

The difference here is in the speed at which you have to manoeuvre. In stronger winds you need to pull the rig up and out of the water with a quicker, more positive jerk. If the rig stays in the water you will move off before you are ready.

Crouch down low and, with back straight, lean back and haul the sail up completely using your body weight and thigh muscles.

Grasp the boom with your front hand and the mast with the other. Twist your upper body towards the nose, then with your front hand pull the rig well across your body before sheeting in with your back hand.

What if . . . the nose keeps turning into the wind as soon as you've sheeted in?

You're not pulling the rig across your body enough before sheeting in. You can also push the nose off the wind with your front foot and pull the tail round with your back foot.

Sailing upwind

● Sail as close to the wind as you can. Find the best angle by turning the nose slowly into and away from the wind until you find the optimum point: usually with the boom about 6-12 ins away from the centreline.

● Daggerboard down to resist the sideways movement of the wind in the sail.

● The windward side of the board may rise: this is known as railing. Move your feet to windward to counterbalance.

● For stronger wind tacking see pages 32-33.

Sailing downwind

● Pull the rig down over your body to reduce wind power.

● Move your weight back as well if you need to, but not too much or the tail will drag in the water slowing you down.

● Daggerboard up to reduce drag and improve stability.

● Shift your feet so that you use bodyweight as well as rig movement when steering (see page 26).

● For stronger wind gybing see pages 34-35.

What if . . .
. . . there's a sudden lull?

If the wind drops suddenly, you need to act quickly to avoid a ducking. Crouch down as low as you can, holding onto the lower mast if necessary, bringing your weight inboard.

What if . . .
. . . a gust of wind hits?

A strong gust can make you go faster if used efficiently. It can also throw you into the water if you're not ready for it! The signs are easy to read: watch for a darker area of rippling water on your windward side. As the gust hits, lean back, bending slightly at the hips to move your weight away from the sail.

Sailing crosswind

● Daggerboard in midway position.
● Move back if you need to but not too far.

Faster tacking

Here are two faster tacks to try in moderate wind. Particularly useful if you want to take up racing later, they involve keeping the sail on the original tack until the board has turned onto its new course, then stepping quickly round the mast.

1

Starting on a close-hauled course, lean the mast well back so that the clew almost touches the water. Put your weight on your back foot, pressing down with your heel to accelerate the turn. The nose will quickly turn towards the wind.

2

As the board turns, grab the mast with your front hand and position your front foot just in front of the mast. Keep your position until the nose of the board has turned right through the wind.

3

Now let go of the boom and quickly step or jump around the mast, swapping your hands over on the mast. At the same time, throw the rig well forward. With practice, you can co-ordinate your jump back and the throw of the rig into one quick, clean movement.

4

With both hands on the boom, lean the mast forward, then sheet in and use your front foot to push the nose off the wind.

Boom to boom tack

This is even quicker since both hands stay on the boom throughout the manoeuvre. But it will need a lot of practice!

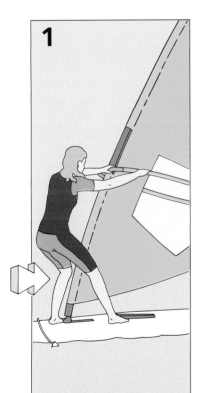

1

2

3

Proceed as in the previous sequence but keep both hands on the boom as the board turns onto its new course, using your feet to push the tail round.

When the nose has turned through the wind, take your back hand off the boom and pass it over your front hand to the other side of the boom.

Then jump round the mast, moving the second hand round to the other side of the boom, and sheet in.

Flare gybe

This is a more advanced and faster gybe for slightly stronger winds. Here a shift of body weight lifts the front of the board and turns it on its tail. It will need lots of practice but is well worth it — the flare gybe is one of the most exhilarating ways of turning the board. As your skill develops, you'll be able to turn the board more and more sharply until it pivots within its own length.

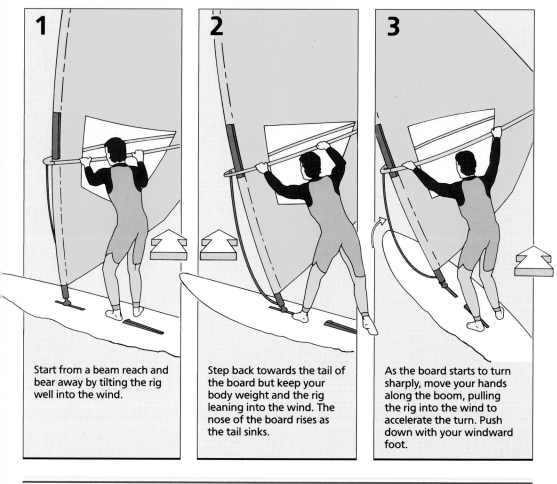

1 Start from a beam reach and bear away by tilting the rig well into the wind.

2 Step back towards the tail of the board but keep your body weight and the rig leaning into the wind. The nose of the board rises as the tail sinks.

3 As the board starts to turn sharply, move your hands along the boom, pulling the rig into the wind to accelerate the turn. Push down with your windward foot.

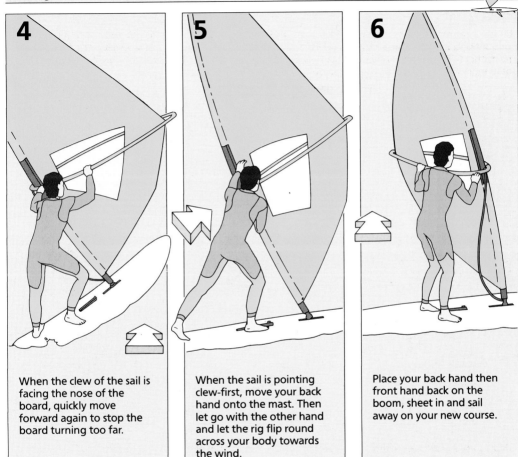

4 When the clew of the sail is facing the nose of the board, quickly move forward again to stop the board turning too far.

5 When the sail is pointing clew-first, move your back hand onto the mast. Then let go with the other hand and let the rig flip round across your body towards the wind.

6 Place your back hand then front hand back on the boom, sheet in and sail away on your new course.

What if . . . the sharpness of the turn makes you overbalance?

Keeping your knees flexed will help you to balance. You can also use your back foot to put pressure on the leeward rail if the turn gets too steep to control.

Using a Harness

A harness is only suitable when you can confidently sail in moderate winds. It provides buoyancy (though it is not a life-saving aid, see page 11) but its main function is to take the strain off your arms so that you can sail comfortably for longer. The harness has a hook in front for lines which you attach to each side of the boom.

There are three kinds of harness available to choose from:

Shoulder/chest harness

Advantages:
● easy to use
● high hook for easy disengaging
● good buoyancy

Disadvantages:
● no support for lower back

Waist harness

Advantages:
● good freedom of movement
● lightweight and comfortable

Disadvantages:
● low buoyancy
● can slip upwards

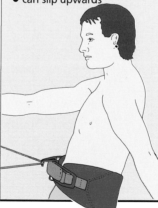

Seat harness

Advantages:
● good lower back support
● very efficient because all your bodyweight can be used to control the rig

Disadvantages:
● low buoyancy
● harder to use at first

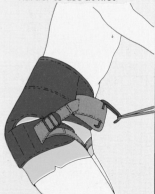

Whichever type you choose, look for:
● comfortable, snug fit   ● maximum support for your lower back   ● a quick-release buckle in case of emergency   ● a spreader bar to reduce pressure on your ribs by spreading the load
● a 'V' shaped 'tangle-free' hook to help prevent tangling of harness lines

Adjusting harness lines

It is vital that you learn to set up the harness lines correctly — you won't be able to control the rig and keep your balance if they are wrong. Practise on dry land until you are sure.

1

Set yourself and the rig as if you are sailing on a beam reach, then take your back hand off the boom. Move the other hand along the boom until you find the balance point where the rig feels weightless.

2

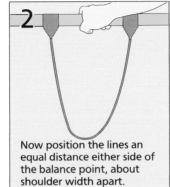

Now position the lines an equal distance either side of the balance point, about shoulder width apart.

Hooking and unhooking

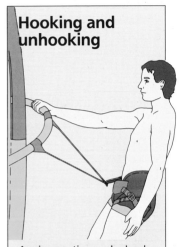

Again, practise on dry land until you can hook in and out without looking. To hook in: from a sailing position, jerk the rig towards you, bending your knees and tilting your hips forward at the same time. The line will flick forwards and should be caught by the hook. To hook out: just pull the boom towards you until the line drops out.

3

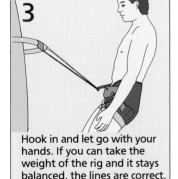

Hook in and let go with your hands. If you can take the weight of the rig and it stays balanced, the lines are correct.

4

Adjust the line length so that you can hook in with your arms almost straight.

What if . . . you want to change direction or stop?

Always unhook first. Otherwise you may well be thrown over the sail. NEVER use the harness when sailing on a run — it is very difficult to control.

Using Footstraps

Almost all boards are fitted with — or have the facility to fit — footstraps. Used properly they give you extra control and make steering in strong winds effortless and fun. But footstraps are only useful when the board is *planing* (see opposite) at speed. Do not try to use them at all until you are sailing very confidently in moderate winds.

Get to know the footstraps

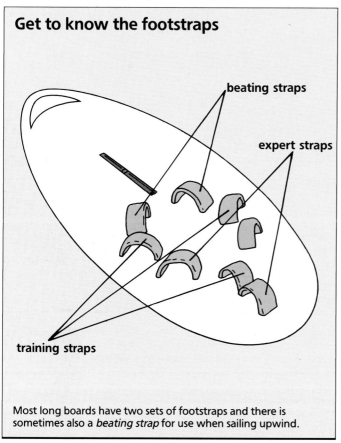

beating straps

expert straps

training straps

Most long boards have two sets of footstraps and there is sometimes also a *beating strap* for use when sailing upwind.

Adjusting the footstraps

You must make sure the straps fit you properly. They should not quite pass over the bridge of your foot. Too tight a fit and your foot won't stay in; too loose and you could twist your ankle. Remove the top cover of the straps and adjust to fit — there is usually a velcro or plastic clip fastening.

When to use the footstraps

Footstraps are mainly used when the wind is sufficient to allow the board to *plane*. The nose lifts slightly and the tail section skims over the surface of the water rather than through it. Planing gives you very fast speeds and is achieved when the board is kept level by correct *trimming* – adjusting your feet to stop the front sinking and the windward edge rising (see page 31).

How to get into the footstraps

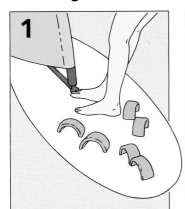

Sail on a reach as fast as you can, daggerboard fully retracted.

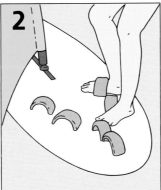

When the board starts to plane, carefully move your front foot into the front strap of the forward set on the windward side. Use your back foot to balance the board.

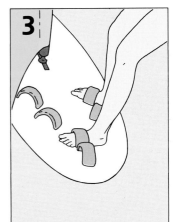

Move your back foot into the front strap of the rear set as your speed increases.

Foot steering

Once your feet are positioned in the straps, you can easily steer with your feet. Put your weight on the windward side by pushing down on your heels to make the board turn into the wind; lean the other way and press on your toes and you will bear away.

What if . . . the wind dies down and the board comes off the plane?

Move your back foot forward again out of the strap to trim the board and regain planing speed.

Beach Start

Hauling the rig up every time you want to get under way is hard work. The beach start is a useful alternative which allows you to get on your board in shallow water, with the rig already up, using the wind to pull you onto the board.

First, learn to control the board . . .

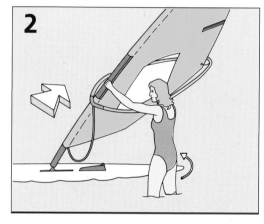

1. Place your front hand on the mast, back hand on the boom. The daggerboard should be partially retracted.

2. Now push down on the mast to make the board turn away from you . . .

3. . . . or pull on it to make it turn towards you. Keep control of the power in the sail by pulling in or easing out with your back hand.

Now for the beach start . . .

1 Position the board on a close reach and move your front hand onto the boom.

2 Place your back foot on the centreline and push the nose away from the wind.

3 Push the boom above you by straightening your arms and the wind will lift the rig upright, pulling you with it.

4 Pull your front foot up and lean the mast forwards to bear away.

What if . . . the sail won't lift you onto the board?

When you straighten your arms (stage 3 above), stretch them as much as you can to get the maximum amount of air into the sail.

What if . . . the board swings into the wind as soon as you try to get your front foot on it?

Press down hard with the rig and with your front foot, and make sure that your back foot is right on the centreline.

UNDERSTANDING THE WIND

A little knowledge of how the wind acts on your sail will help you improve your windsurfing skills. It's certainly much easier to solve problems if you understand what is actually happening and why.

Two terms you need to understand are the *centre of effort* (CE) and the *centre of lateral resistance* (CLR). The CE is the point on the sail where the air pressure is greatest and the most lift is generated. The CLR is the point on the board where resistance to the sideways movement is greatest (if you were standing in the water you could push the board sideways at this point without either end turning – think of it as the pivot point of a see-saw).

Steering

In practice you know that tilting the rig makes you turn – but how does it work?

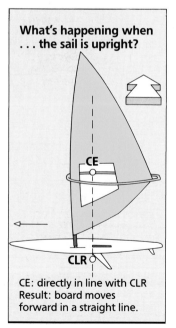

What's happening when . . . the sail is upright?

CE: directly in line with CLR
Result: board moves forward in a straight line.

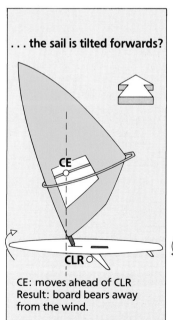

. . . the sail is tilted forwards?

CE: moves ahead of CLR
Result: board bears away from the wind.

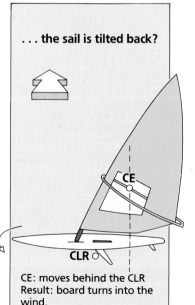

. . . the sail is tilted back?

CE: moves behind the CLR
Result: board turns into the wind.

The Wind in the Sail

A sail works rather like the wing of an aeroplane, but whereas air flowing over an aircraft wing generates an upward force or lift, the force on a sail generates forward propulsion.

1 As the air meets the sail, it separates to pass either side. The curve of the sail makes the air flow more slowly on the windward side of the sail, since it has less distance to travel. The different speeds result in an area of high pressure on the windward side, and low pressure on the leeward.

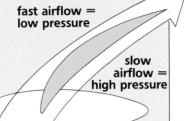

fast airflow = low pressure

slow airflow = high pressure

Apparent wind

Apparent wind is the wind you actually feel when sailing. It is a combination of the *true wind* (what you'd feel if you were standing still) and the *head wind* created by the forward movement of the board. The apparent wind will seem to come from further in front than the true wind, and the faster you go, the greater this effect is. As you pick up speed, you will have to sheet in further to keep the sail at maximum power.

2 The sail is sucked into the low pressure area on the leeward side. The board cannot move sideways very much because of the combined resistance of the daggerboard, the board itself and your body. Instead, pressure builds up and the board moves forwards.

sail is drawn into low pressure area

3 If the sail is not angled correctly to the wind, the air flow breaks up and becomes turbulent and the board will slow down.

undersheeting: turbulent leeward flow

oversheeting: turbulent windward flow

Identifying Wind and Tides

Always check the wind and weather before you go windsurfing to make sure you can cope with the conditions – dangerous mistakes can be avoided with a little common sense. Here are some general guidelines:

- Get into the habit of checking the weather reports in newspapers and on the television and radio.

- Wind direction is as important as wind strength. Beginners should NEVER sail if there is an offshore wind. Lick your finger and hold it up, or hold up a handkerchief, to help you determine wind direction if there are no flags or other obvious signs around.

- Check times and heights of tides.

Tides

Tides are caused by the gravitational pull of the moon and sun and change gradually from day to day. The tide takes about six hours to change from high to low and its pull is strongest during the middle two hours. The strongest tides – known as spring tides – occur just after the full and new moons. NEVER sail in an outgoing spring tide – if the wind dropped you would be swept out to sea.

Times and heights of tides are displayed in tide tables in newspapers, newsagents and chandlers in coastal towns.

Tide in or out?

If you can't find a tide table, look for these signs:

- WET sand on the beach means the tide is going out.

- DRY sand on the beach means the tide is coming in.

- Look at any boats that are anchored nearby. Unless the wind is very strong, they will have turned themselves to face the direction of the tide.

- Look at buoys and beacons: can you see bow waves or wake around them? These will indicate which way the stream is flowing past them.

- Are there any warning flags or signs about tides or currents? Always heed them.

See also Safety Sense, pages 12-13.

The Beaufort Scale

This is the most commonly used scale of wind strengths.

Force	Description	Signs on the sea	Signs on land	Wind speed less than	Symbol
0	Calm	Mirror-smooth surface	Smoke rises vertically	1 knot	
1	Light air	Ripples but no foam crests	Smoke drifts with wind	1-3 knots	
2	Light breeze	Small wavelets with smooth crests	Wind felt on face	4-6 knots	
3	Gentle breeze	Large wavelets with crests starting to break	Leaves and small twigs moving. Light flags will be extended	7-10 knots	
4	Moderate	Small waves becoming longer; fairly frequent white horses	Dust and loose paper are lifted; small branches move	11-16 knots	
5	Fresh breeze	Moderate waves with frequent white horses	Small trees sway; waves on lakes inland	17-21 knots	
6	Strong breeze	Large waves start to form; spray likely	Large trees moving; whistling in telephone wires; difficult to use umbrellas	22-27 knots	
7	Near gale	Sea heaps up; and white foam from breaking waves blows with the wind	Whole trees bend; quite hard to walk against the wind	28-33 knots	
8	Gale	Moderately high, long waves; well-defined streaks of foam	Twigs break off trees; difficult to walk	34-40 knots	
9	Severe gale	High waves; dense foam streaks; crests roll over	Branches break off trees	41-47 knots	

Going Further: Windsurfing Specialisations

The specialised forms of windsurfing offer exciting possibilities once you can confidently handle the board through all the basic manoeuvres covered in this book. You can learn a great deal from watching and talking to more experienced windsurfers, joining a club, taking advanced and specialist courses and reading some of the excellent books available on the subject. Meanwhile, here is a small taster to whet your appetite.

Freestyle

This basically means performing stunts on your board, which is great fun and good for impressing your friends! Most freestyle tricks need calm water and a force 2-3 wind and you'll need to wear a wetsuit to protect yourself from grazes and bumps as well as to keep warm.

Some of the easiest tricks to pick up include:

- sailing with your back to the rig
- kneeling or lying on your board
- spinning round in a pirouette on the ball of your foot
- leaning back so that your head dips in the water
- and riding along on the rail instead of the deck.

Watch the experts, ask how it's done and then have a go!

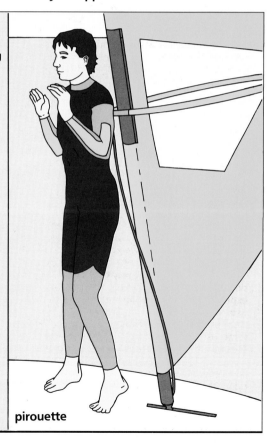

pirouette

Wavesailing and wave jumping

Sailing the waves is one the most exciting aspects of the sport, but you shouldn't attempt it as a beginner. As you get more expert, you will first need to learn a variety of gybes and other techniques for strong winds. You will also need the right equipment — there are boards and rigs specially designed for wavesailing.

Even more daring are the spectacular wave jumps which expert windsurfers can perform with such apparent ease. Of course it should never be attempted by relative beginners, but as something to aspire to later it certainly wins on the excitement stakes!

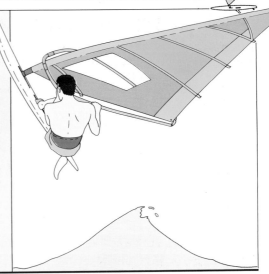

Racing and competitions

Course racing, speedsailing and other windsurfing events take place internationally, nationally and locally. If you can get to see a major regatta, you will find it both exciting and informative. On a local level, taking part in competitions is the best way to improve your skills. You will meet other enthusiasts, pick up expert tips and have opportunities to try out new venues.

Course racing involves several races around the same, usually 'W' or triangular-shaped, course. Competitors are awarded points according to their placings in each circuit. In speedsailing competitions, competitors race against the clock down the fixed distance of a straight-reaching leg.

Glossary

APPARENT WIND The wind you feel as you sail along. A combination of TRUE WIND and wind created by your forward movement.

BACK HAND/FOOT The hand or foot nearer to the tail of the board.

BALANCE POINT The point at which the rig feels weightless.

BEAM REACH A course where the board travels directly across the wind.

BEAR AWAY To steer away from the wind.

BEATING Sailing upwind.

BEATING STRAP Footstrap for use when sailing upwind.

BROAD REACH A diagonal downwind course.

CENTRE OF EFFORT (CE) The point on the sail where the air pressure is greatest.

CENTRE OF LATERAL RESISTANCE (CLR) The point on the board where resistance to sideways movement is greatest.

CLEAT Small device for securing a line.

CLOSE-HAULED A diagonal upwind course, as close to the wind as possible.

CLOSE REACH A diagonal upwind course between a broad reach and close hauled.

DOWNWIND A point ahead of you when the wind is behind you.

EASE OUT See SHEET OUT.

FRONT HAND/FOOT The hand or foot nearer to the nose of the board.

GYBE To turn the tail of the board through the wind — see also TACK.

HEAD WIND Wind created by your own speed.

LEEWARD Anything downwind of a given object. The leeward side of the board is the side away from the wind — see also WINDWARD.

LUFF To steer into the wind.

NO GO ZONE Area of 45° on each side of the wind where it is impossible to sail.

OFFSHORE WIND Wind blowing away from the shore.

ONSHORE WIND Wind blowing onto the shore.

PLANING Sailing fast, with the tail of the board skimming over rather than ploughing through the water.

PORT The left side of the board looking towards the nose — see also STARBOARD.

RAILING A rising of the windward side of the board.

RIGGING Setting up the mast, sail and boom.

RUN A course with the wind directly behind.

SAILING POSITION Basic position for sailing with both hands on the boom and body leaning slightly back.

SECURE POSITION Stable, static position of the board, sail and sailor.

SHEET IN To pull the sail towards you.

SHEET OUT To let the sail out.

STARBOARD The right side of the board looking towards the nose — see also PORT.

TACK (verb) To turn the nose of the board through the wind — see also GYBE.

TRIM THE BOARD To position your feet correctly on the board to keep it level or at any required angle.

TRIM THE SAIL To adjust the position of the rig by SHEETING in or out to gain maximum power from the sail.

TRUE WIND The wind you feel when standing still — see also APPARENT WIND.

UPHAUL (verb) To pull up the rig.

UPWIND A point ahead of you when you are facing into the wind.

WINDWARD Anything upwind of a given object: the windward side of the board is the side nearer to the wind — see also LEEWARD.

(See pages 6-7 for parts of the rig and board).

Printed in Italy